An Invisible Accordion

Acknowledgements:
Peter Baltensperger's ''Thirsting'' was first published in the HMS Press Broadsheet Series #2; p.j. flaming's ''Drive to Canmore'' is reprinted from *voir dire* (Broken Jaw Press); I. B. Iskov's ''election day or uncle bobby'' was previously published in *Outreach Connection Newsletter;* Susan Ioannou's ''Watching The Young'' was previously published in *Other Voices*; Anne F. Walker's ''Winter Poem # 1 (the cloaked woman)'' was previously published in *Pregnant Poems* (Black Moss Press). All of these poems are reprinted by permission of the authors. We apologize for the omission of any other acknowledgements which should appear here.

Published by
Broken Jaw Press
Box 596 Stn A   SAN 1171437
Fredericton NB E3B 5A6   Ph   506 454·5127
Canada   Fax 506 452·8565   E·mail jblades@nbnet.nb.ca

Manuscript typing by Rebecca Flewelling
Cover photo and book design by Joe Blades

Printed and bound in Canada by Sentinel Printing, Yarmouth, Nova Scotia
September 1995

Canadian Cataloguing in Publication Data
Main entry under title:

An invisible accordion

    ISBN 0-921411-38-3

1. Canadian poetry (English) – 20th century. * I. Footman, Jennifer, 1942- II. Canadian Poetry Association.

PS8279.I68 1995   C811'. 5408   C95-950228-9
PR9195.7.I68 1995

An Invisible Accordion

A Canadian Poetry Association Anthology

Jennifer Footman

Editor

Broken Jaw Press

Fredericton · Canada

An Invisible Accordion

Introduction to the poems in the first Canadian Poetry Association Anthology

It is a great honour to be asked to edit this material. Seldom does an editor have such a variety of work to consider and such a very rich selection from which to pick. It has been a real pleasure going through the material selected by each poet and trying to find poems which work together and have some kind of narrative through the selection. It's as if I now know all the members, in all their varied lives, through their poems.

My feeling is that an anthology of this type is here to represent every one of the varied voices of the people who belong to the Canadian Poetry Association. Some voices have been silent up to now and this is our chance of sharing their magic; some voices have been heard all over Canada and other parts of the world. It is this mixture of voices within the Canadian Poetry Association which gives it the warm and welcoming face it presents.

The subjects have been as varied as the voices. Many, many poems about death and loss. And what can move us more than death and loss? I have tried to balance this with a good selection of the more positive observations on life. Street life. Angel life. Family life. Some poems just for a laugh. And we all need laughs.

The forms are as varied as the material, from the very formal to the totally unformed. Long. Short.

I don't feel it fair or appropriate to mention any particular poet or poem because it would be impossible to mention them all.

In here there is a poem for every occasion and for every voice. I have been told by students in the many schools I teach that they hate poetry, man, do they hate poetry. I try to convince them and show them that there is a poet for every reader and for every taste. Just as some of us like to wear green and some blue so there is a shade of poem for everyone.

Some poets and critics say that anthologies have the fault of not giving enough meat to see one through the meal. For me this is an advantage. Flicking through an anthology I often find the new voice that intrigues, fascinates or just annoys. Sometimes I stumble across a poet who teases my imagination to the degree I have to buy his/her book and get to know the voice better. This is how I see an anthology. And if that poet doesn't have a book and still that poetry intrigues then perhaps the reader can write to that poet and ask them about a book. It was through anthologies I found Sharon Olds, Lorna Crozier, Milton Acorn. Picking through an anthology the reader can stray from the heavy to the light, from the dense to the feathery. Another thing I find so appropriate and interesting in this selection is that just about every kind of hyphenated Canadian is represented. Some of the people I do know and some information is from the bios and sometimes I'm guessing from the names. It is also satisfying to see that every age group from the very young to the very old is here too. Above all an anthology has to be fun. if it isn't fun then why read it? I do hope this material from the members of the Canadian Poetry Association is fun to read. It was for me.

– Jennifer Footman
June 1995

dedicated in memorium to

Milton Acorn

Herb Barrett

Shaunt Basmajian

Jones

Katherine Kostyniuk

John Patrick

David ''Rhino'' Reid

Dorothy Cameron Smith

John B. Lee

The Clifting of Sacred Cows

Some sacred cows it seems
will have their secret dreams of flight confirmed
by leaping from the high cliffs that sheer above the Irish sea
for instance
they might be seen
wildly flapping their big-boned hocks
like huge blue ladies and mutant angels
who flack madly falling from the sky
beatified kye that come by sevens cattling down the air
like da Vinci's impossible machines
materializing above the crashing waters
with balloon basket jetsam
and all the other disposable beasts of the supernumerary flying
arc
called earth
because if the wind dies
the candle lives
to light the way of loss
where any poor man knows the cost
of a rich man's philosophy
when it comes to death.

Bernadette Dyer

Star Boys in J.A.

The evening, thick with crickets.
Frogs and mosquitos give rise to ragged newspaper boys
Who shout ''*Star*!'' into the humid Kingston air.
They lean in at car windows,
Blue black neck veins pumped up
From wanting the unattainable,
And their cheeks rounded
With lush Bombay and St. Julian seeds
That cannot disguise their melancholy eyes
Stained with dried blood tears
Of shame and regrets
Which seems to salivate even from the rusty zinc shacks
That totter on the verge of collapse at road's edge.
And the hissing sounds made in the *Star* boy's husky throats
Echoes disconsolately, electrifying our attention,
And obliterates ragged sleeves,
Exposed knees, and inconsolable hopelessness.

Hope Morritt

To Etienne

like your gliders
you are slip-streaming
beyond the sullen bonds
of earth where dreams
twinkle in galaxies of stars
the science-fiction world
beckoning – challenges
shooting like frenzied comets
all there in the cosmos
for you to catch and court in
the never-never land of tomorrow

Kathy Fretwell

A Paranoid Switch

Howls, half-vowels
assault
my plugged ears,
thoughts slime down
dark mews,
bedsheets writhe
in a bedlam rag,
pillows mold
strange hollows

This crazed almost comic
discord is darkly shadowed:
Is that girlchild voice
which squeaked, Rhino!
while huge daddy horned me
recovering volume?
Is my daughter's own
moaned bodily harm
overpowering the thickness
of night's lidded eye?

At naptime
my dim lens
fix on the fan
still plugged in,
churning months
of smokedazed
nightmarish
questions
I yank out the cord
Auditory seizures
disconnect

Rosemary Hollingshead

I've Just Finished Writing a Letter

I've just finished writing a letter
to my brother telling him I've been
officially medically diagnosed as being
legally blind, aware that the sight of me
with a seeing eye dog would impress him more
than any words I could use as he's always
preferred animals his horses and dogs to me
but then again he might take pride that
his sister he'd despaired of for so long
is finally being eyed in respectable legal
terms in her community

Peggy Fletcher

Lorraine

Even in her dying
he upstages her
his heart is really in for it
his fear
triggers old alarms
summons abandoned loyalties
to play audience
to the latest/last performance?

Grey, swollen
without the strength to argue
she is pale director
to this awful scene
its backdrop of black curtains
swallowing light
into post-medicated oblivion.

Gail Sidonie Sobat

Grandview

some grieve publicly
I cannot
and perhaps that is why
I visit these granite giants
stare at their immobile stony faces
crevassed with pain

I am this glacial tarn
chill and icily unapproachable
unfathomable and disconsolate

I am this lichen
clinging to life on a barren stone
exposed to the elements, but ever-enduring

I am this waterfall
my tears roaring sorrow
eternally outpouring grief

here I walk with giants
stroke their sad faces
listen to their age-old stories
hold the past tightly to my breast

Maynard Luterman

A Kind Death

The angel of death kisses my father
And his soul triumphantly returns home
Selfishly we gather to mourn our loss
Listening to stories of another time forgotten
In the kitchen my father is being deified
His memory being polished like a silver lamp
While on the ward his friends wither
Barely holding on to life
Their dignity being stripped
Like old paint from an antique
Until the rotten wood,
Exposed so it can no longer hide
Unrecognizable shivers and splinters
A living memory of a proud structure that once stood
He knew to leave
Before the music stopped
The decorations taken down and the ballroom cleaned
I can see his smile now.
His way of telling me he knew best
Death was kind to him and cruel to me
I wanted so badly to say I love you
Before he said good-bye.

Suzanne Fitz-Andrews

City Nights

Silver light scars the wrist
A bangled lady
Jangles.

Broken, patchworked lives
Over-emphasized
Are looking for love
In dirty bars.
Finding only smoke-ringed dreams.

Gin-cracked laughter echoes
Whiskey smiles.
Across the counter
The barman watches.

The air, thick with fiction
Tells many stories.
An old man shuffles loneliness
Out the door
And the lady gives the night
Her empty words.

Beryl Baigent

The Tao of Knowing

To commit oneself is to
have perceived commitment
between the lines in childhood
the steadiness maintained
underneath the unsteadiness.
                    – Joan Finnigan

Some parts of the journey
Can only be taken
Alone
Down the spiral staircase
Out into the extraneous
Air
Via the watery course
Swimming towards the threshold:
The birth.

And in the final quest
For everlasting light
No-one
Calms the waves
Provides the celestial music   yet
In between
Guides are positioned at
Strategic points along the
Causeway

And when you dive deep
Into the fathomless unknown
Mermaids
Of your own imagination
Chant womansong   share
Energy
And steer you through the shoals
And caves of unconsciousness.
Mirrors

In mermaid-hands reflect your image
The beauty and confusion of
Relationships
The duality of the endless sea
Which gives and takes away
Absorbs
Then tosses up its treasure
Onto populous beaches and dark
Shores.

There Earth Spirits tell you
Their own living tales and
Wait
In case you should need to lean
On their animal instincts or be
Comforted
By warm bodies and unquestioning adoration.
And always you'll know the commitment of
The Old Ones

As you climb to the highest peak
And sometimes miss a foothold
Always
A hand will be there to carve
Another niche to steady the swinging
Rope.
And you will press on with eyes
Wide open and the fire of your heart
                    Creating.

                                        – Christmas 1990

Jill Battson

A Morphine Headache

Shout there is of Portuguese
rattling through the kitchen
and behind that closed semi gloss
latex newly painted door
a chosen grey
the billowy softness
of death impending
knocking of rosary beads
tacky mucus rattle
in the throat
dice players on the road to death
and how much do you charge
for snowblowing
speak louder
you paid too much
and she is toxic yellow brown
skeletal remains
with an ocean view
and know I do still you
I do

swallow it
just one draught
and you will be talking
listening I am to them
at my age I don't give a fuck
cloying urine turns thick
ahh
the bed under sometimes it gets stuck
in the light so I can see you
kiss me
in a room of ceramic pigs
she is soft focus delirium

Fisher Price alarm baby crackles
we cut morphine with valium
up and down
sleep and talk
hand still blood warm with
pressure of heat cheek on lips
air kisses breathless in my ear
there is no depth to the horror
Jill it's only
hug me
there it is – I can never do more

Bernice Lever

Hurting You

Hurting you was never
part of my plan
I never meant –
what I said was –
this doesn't mean that –
I was trying to hurt you,
Saying "sorry" never helps,
is no excuse nor solution –
Sorry is a useless bandaid
always slipping off and
never helping to heal hurt –
What I said wasn't intended
to hurt you,
it wasn't directed at
you personally,
just a passing observation
that I did mean,
well, but not to be painful –
I never meant to hurt you
at first   but now
I do, I do!

Wayne Ray

Hoarfrost

Milkweed pods and golden rod, their
hoarfrost melted by the sunrise
along gravel roads that have seen
many a raven's midnight wing.
Just leeside of the frost and
as far as the eye can see at dawn,
the silhouette of a million pea seeds
hung in their pre-harvest wombs
trail shadows with this day's sun.

So quiet you can hear the wind passing
over the last raven's wings as it
lands, talons crunching the soil
a distance away. Waiting and watching.

The sun breaks into daylight
above a hill, warming the good Earth,
the road less travelled and two
night weary travellers.

Pulling a bent leg to her chest
on the warm hood of the car at roadside
she shades her eyes as the morning light
changes from a cool orange to a warmer yellow.
She's watching her dream lover stride
out into the farmer's field with his heart
in one hand and their future in the other.

He turns towards her and sings his song,
ravens rise in the morning air,
starlings land at her feet, she smiles,
catches his love one word at a time,
closes her eyes for a sunshine second,
breathes deeply to calm pre-dawn fears,
slides off the hood and back inside
travelling the road less travelled, alone.

The note on the small box beside her read:
Come to me my lady white
just after dawn in early light
with this ring as a compass we shall start
to rewrite the map of the human heart.

Road dust settled on raven's wings.
Goldenrod less golden for a furlong.
Pea pods became corn husks and wheat fields
and the tires of her car spit stones
as she headed East for the coast,
the rising sun burning his memory in her tears.

The fear of a forever love is stronger
than the fear of friendship, she thought.
The dust collected on the grass
and the hoarfrost would be the only thing returning.

Margaret Joy Borle

Watching the Snow Fall

Watching
the snow
fall
from darkened skies,
I remember your tears
and the way
your eyes clouded
with the knowledge
of death.

You wept for years
barren of love
knowing too late
a lifetime
is too long
to live in isolation.

Days shortened
by clouds
and the coming of night.

Your tears
falling on my hand
attempted to cover
refuse of years.

I need
the absolution
of drifting snow.

Mary Lou Doyon

Richard, as Seen by an Admiring Friend

Along the side I watched him pass,
His forward sway has proved to last,
  All through my life there has never been
Such a caring, trustworthy and honourable friend.

Without hesitation he would be by my side,
Sarah, Michael and Paul – the centre of his pride,
  "Forever young," hints his elfin smile,
As he speaks – his kindness – is felt – all the while.

Flaw-seeking eyes are never with him,
The light of our friendship will never grow dim,
  My aching heart his presence consoles,
His comforting aura seeps into my soul.

Where shallow rivers flow, he will not be found,
His hair and friendly advice always extremely sound,
  There is no room in his life for hate,
The one he chooses will be a very lucky mate.

For many years he has come to cook,
Sometimes late – but with just a look
  He can soften my heart – oh what a winner,
Dab of sauce – dash of wine – and we have – 'ah' dinner.

Richard, darkness is not in my thoughts of you,
Your spirit is shown in your crinkly eyes of blue,
  As sure as comes the dawning of Spring,
He cares for you as His birds on the wing!

Carla Campoli

Whisper softly
in my ear
and tell me
why I need you.

The warm touch
of your fingers
slide down my back
and capture emotions
and hidden thoughts
unknown to the mind.

Swimming through
the blue of eyes
and taking in the heat
ocean waves
of lust and greed
crash against my soul.

And those among you
laugh and sing
so merrily
each day
and we
as fragile
as we are
bleed in the wind.

Mary Chryssoulakis

Inner Child

He's muttering –
angry that he has to shovel
the damned stuff again.

I look out the window
on a meringue world
glittering in bright winter sun.

An old excitement builds in me.

Smooth untrodden white
begs for angels.
Softly moulded hills and valleys
evoke a memory of my wooden sled,
honey-hued with bright red runners.
Sun-softened snow,
just right for packing,
becomes great forts
with snowball ammunition.

A time of exciting spills
breathless laughter –
chewing snow beads
stuck to woollen mittens and
a wonderful sensual thrill
of being brushed
head to toe
with Mother's broom.

With Hellenic gloom he shovels
a fierce attack on his enemy,
my friend...a pity

he never was a child in winter.

Mary Partridge

Divorce Proceedings

Across the room   two hirelings
in three piece pinstripe   debate
while we hold duplicate copies
of legalese & quiet conversation

Gold pens tap on tempered glass
silk neckties chafe
as our empty nest is torn apart
twig by twig   on paper

Countless coffees
      a couple of crullers
            & a cheese-twist later
they agree upon what we agreed upon
      courtly handshakes are exchanged
            & the exit pointed out

Since we shared   you & I
more than children & the deed to a house
we can stand warm in winter's doorway

I lift your collar against the cold
you steady me down icy steps
      then good sense takes us
                        in opposite directions

Bob Ezergailis

She is Vain

she is vain
and I want
to be the dress
that clings
everywhere tight
to her body
to caress teasingly
at her thighs
knowing the feel
of every part of her
all day long
to be the brassiere
holding her breasts
to be the stockings
hugging her legs
and as satin
sheets
to know the feel
of her nakedness
all night long.

– October 19, 1994

Susan Ioannou

Watching The Young

(For Anita Krumins)

I want to lick them
   with my eyes,
feel that old purr
   rumble to a start,
rub my face
   against the glow
illuminating perfect skin.

Their smoothness
   warms me.
Their easy swaying
   into unison
is forgotten body music
   I long for,
feel echo in my angles
   when I watch.

He is a peach, fuzz-ripe.
   She, the polished apple.
They swell round and firm
   without knowing
a twig dangles them
   over the abyss.

That is their beauty to me:
   innocence,
just beyond time's claws.

Jill Meriel Fox

Wavelength

I can finish your sentences
You can start my laugh

I can read your dreams
You can touch my mood

Wordless communication
    incarnate by
intangible sensibilities

Without touching
I hold you

With bonding
You free me

You are the gift
I give
    to myself

Carmen Ziolkowski

Peacock Feathers

We don't know each other
no language fills the void –
your urgencies are not mine.

When you leave my warm bed
my universe expands
from white linen
I smooth away the outline of your body –

I straighten out the pillow
with its peacock embroidery
soften the eiderdown
brushing away the echo of
your blasphemies –

You might return
the colour of my skin
is unchanged.

Anne F. Walker

Winter Poem # 1 (the cloaked woman)

On this first day of
snow staying on the ground,
     even though it is nothing but
a gently, homy, stay-inside feeling
I know sometime I'll remember it as our first snowdown together.

The smell of someone smoking inside
and the shutness
of windows.

The cloaked woman came out tonight.

Albert W. J. Harper

Absence

Your answer is forever hidden
Secret in its silences
Unspoken in words
You are everywhere for me
Without appearing.

I will see you in my dreams
Entering from the hallway
Filling the room with your presence
It is empty with your absence.

You make life for all time
Rid of its hollow moments
Each spent day torn from the wall
Lost to love's paradox
That will not come undone.

No answer to my call
Spells sorrow
The dream returns unquenched
In the hidden self
That is yourself,

Yet all such loss is less
Than loss of love's ideal
There is no loss
In love that waits for me.

Melvin Robert Appell

My Faith

My faith
don't ask me why
is so easily shaken.
Like ripe fruit
rotten apples
it falls
to the ground
with the first
adverse winds
that blow.
Where others get
their tenacity
I'll never know.

Rosemary Aubert

Mabel at the Table

Then there was the day you got mad
over lunch at Mabel Dodge.

One of those golden days
country leaves crisp as a pie.
French breeze cools the soup.
I'm sitting in her husband Edwin's chair
across from her
and she looks up.

All I did was not turn away
all I did was let the light arc
like Edison
all I did was look and see
how beautiful she was.
How beautiful she was:
when I smiled at her,
it was as though I were looking
in a mirror for the first time
and I always like what I see
in a mirror.

But you, sparrow, you bird, you Alice
jumped up like a popped chestnut
whoosh out the door onto the terrace
your brown dress just another one of
those leaves.

How could you be hurt by just a look?
Is that a word? Is that a touch or
some kind of promise? No.
Well, listen, I *did* promise didn't I?
Never to do it again
never ever do it
never
never again
never ever again, little Alice
never again until next time.

Estelle McLachlan

The Fairy Ring

Bad luck omens
sprouting like weeds
seized and gripped you
strangleholding.

Sleek cat, night black
save for his long green eyes
moved from your shuddering touch
his warm silk beauty.

Boots on the table, crossed knives
touched wood, spilled salt
13th Fridays and broken mirrors...
I laughed at you
Walking with you
mocked you
darted under your sinister ladders
toed, gleefully, the cracks...

Yet I remember the fairy ring
you showed me
in our morning garden
crystal with dew
two believers
our time of light, Mother
and a strange magic.

Only later could I understand
your dread of casual guarantees
of second hurt, of happiness
that might evaporate
as once before.

Only later, understand
that in the garden
by the tender circle
the magic was, simply
the mute and helpless love
deep in our hearts.

Heather Tisdale-Nisbet

Worth the Fear

It's worth the fear
to get above timberline,
look down on fir forests;
not watching for
but driving over fallen rocks;
to emerge at Paradise
with cotton mouth and rubber legs,
gasp in the pure air
tilt your head back to see
the monolith of snow and rock,
then get a book about all the people
who reached the summit
and the others who
fainted, fell down, froze,
died the way they wanted to.

Lini Richarda Grol

New Life...

A sudden
burst of bright light
and the exuberant call
of a small bird,
came into my sombre room
and quite unexpectedly
weaving golden threads
in the unfinished work
on my too long
silent loom.

Isabel Sturgeon

Words Endure

There's fire in the words
      of life and love, of sorrow.
I toss my words on moonbeams
      to mingle with the wise.
Pen my thoughts to let them float
      far on the sea of life.
Words solidify the past
      to futures in disguise.

Adele Kearns Thomas

Circumstances of Spring

Winter limps
leans wearied
on bedridden arrangement
drained shell
crack-shrivels
like blind fingers
mantis-like
choreographing sketch
feels composure
of earth's coolness
twist of winter.

Darlene Spong Henderson

The Girl With Peacock Hair

The girl with peacock hair
stayed out all night
worrying her mama.
Her feathers are bright
like the cock's not the hen's.
She runs
down cavernous alleys behind restaurants
where elegant people entertain.
At first she thinks it's an adventure.
Cool fresh breezes caress her runaway skin.
The twilight sky dancing
with Northern Lights smiles upon her.

The girl with peacock hair
sparkles like a jewel
within her naivete
in contrast with the tired residents
of the inner city.
As the night wears on
and she drags her tired self
beneath the neon tapestries
and fends off men who want a young toy
she thinks of how she is
worrying her mama.

Gerry Stewart

Spirit

The spirit survives
its changing form, like seeds sown in autumn
anticipating
the promise of flowers blooming in spring.

Or a chance wind
sweeping starlings to flight, to grasp at life
to flake the air like soot
the ambiguity of then and now confused.

The present etches
the surface like riddles scribbled in sand,
the past burnished
with pain illuminates the future.

Seeking solitude
transcending time and space, spirit embraces
life in all its forms
the earth, the waves, the flames of the universe.

Martha Attema

to be one with the waves

to be one with the waves
just at the point where they break and
roll to the shore
to be a wave and move with crashing sound onto the rocks
break the man-made dikes in heavy storms
to be a gentle wave   embrace children people
watch their splashful play in sun-filled days

to be one with the waves
just at the point where they break and
roll to the shore
to go with the tide as long as the world turns
watch seagulls dive for their wave-hidden meal
as fish swim for safety   hide in watery spray
carry seashells gently onto the beach

to be one with the waves
just at the point where they break and
roll to the shore
yesterday's worries   tomorrow's fears
roll onto the beach in never-ending rhythm
deadlines   responsibilities crash onto the shore
frustrations   anger hit the dike time after time

to be one with the waves
just at the point where they break and
roll to the shore
the wind is my partner   lover
we play catch and hide when in the mood
touch with feathery touch when tired
lose control in angry storms

to be one with the waves
just at the point where they break and roll to the shore

Sheila Hyland

Meditation in May

Do you miss the sea air?
The mist over the mountains
The salty taste of the breeze
The wind tangling your hair
The constant walk
On an empty shore
Do you remember you were here?

Recall: windburn
From walking the pier
Candy-rock, wrapped pink on white
Lettering going right through
Like water in a pipe
Eating ice-cream cornets
From the tricycle man
To keep hunger at bay
Till we landed in to a feast
Of shrimp and mussels
Do you miss the sea air?

Hilton McCully

Sea Gull

No friend of mine
   Rips open garbage
      Early Thursday morning

Decorates unoffending
   Cherry red car
      In driveway

      But
Now injured Sea Gull
   Flops around at side
      Of street

      As
I await animal patrol
   While cold drizzle falls
      On injured Sea Gull
         Needing friend

Penny L. Ferguson

Humpbacks

I see them first as shadows
beneath the boat
and am reminded of salmon
laying in deep, cold pools
beneath the footbridge
of my childhood.
The depth here, I can only imagine
and I realize they appear yards long,
even fathoms below.

My breath catches as they rise
and their features become clear –
white on black,
barnacles like clusters of light
against darkness.
They glide carefully
inches beneath our hull,
to just break the surface
on the other side,
people watching –
great black icebergs
showing only their noses,
their one tenth.

I hold my breath
and wish to be suspended
in this moment,
to be forever free,
forever in awe of their beauty,
forever on the water with the whales.

Lynn Tait

Akumel to Genesis

A forty-five minute walk, says our guide.
He lied.

Surrounded by poisonous trees
        and their antidotes
Abandoned wasp nests overhead
        grin like fat, paper cats.

Turbulent, rock earth trail
        gives way to Padro's farm
Stick structures   dirt floors
        patch quilt of corn stalks
                        citrus trees
            corn stalks

Long-eared cattle
        nose Padro
            like pet goats
        looking for handouts.

Wife washes clothes in old basin
We fantasize
        she hides the "Maytag"
            till we pass.

Further on – an underwater cave
Slipping into
        snorkel gear and cold water
Enter rock cathedral
        so not to disturb
            some ongoing mass.

Bats hang, wide-eyed
        startled parishioners doing penance.

Our flashlights
      church candles casting shadows
We blow them out together.

The earth is void and without form
We are the first stirrings of life
Clay dolls touched by God
Breathing in
      black water silence.

p.j. flaming

Drive to Canmore

On the drive to canmore i only half listen to your stories about tugboats and sea
It is the land that has me spellbound now
Breath in heart resting riding on the gusty winds and snow blown roads
One sharp curve rocks the boat
Out on the ice covered lake i see *your* stories your legacy
Your response to the suitcase we found this morning tattered and bursting
Full of sketches letters drawings heart throbs and mother's "most pleasant memories"

Long before you two ever met
mother was an innocent mooning over Harry James under the wide warm southern alberta skies
You were a gangly young tar before your time
"Because I was big" you say "they thought I was 19"
Tugging the sea up and down the coast from sitka to san francisco

Before i hear the ending   i start to hold the beginning
of memories & mountains & mixed metaphors & even before the lines are
w/rote these poems are
my stories
my legacy
to whomever will need to know these things

Guna Ikona

Obsession

I want to be kissed
by a killer whale
(his big pink tongue
caressing my soft cheek)
like he does it on TV
in Niagara:
   the girl glowing,
   her giggles – tiny silver bells
   over the sun-splashed water.
This beast
tender and huge
matching the grandeur
in distance glimpsed Falls,
his mouth's wide smile
with its 44 sharp teeth.

That wish now
overpowers all other
romantic inklings
in the down-to-earth
unremarkable life-size
human togetherness.

Big body glistening
in a black and white formal attire –
a seven-foot long streamlined elegance,
seen over and over again
flashing on the screen.

Fulfilment!
(One thrill seeking sparrow
crosses the road
of a speeding car.)
But what, if he shortens my nose,
fancies my fingers as bite-size carrots,
cuts the jugular vein?
It is a mammal, a rocket, a superfish
dousing us with water
as it flicks its tail with delight
in farewell.

Hazel Birt

The Grecian Cats

The Grecian Cats prowl
                    everywhere
they meet the tourist ships
                    and watch
from tree and wall in case
                    a crumb would
fall or cheese or fish.

They sun themselves
                    on ancient tombs
cats love the Parthenon,
                    they play
with pigeons in the square
                    and haunt
the market stalls.

Lean tough and fierce
                    they come in
tabby stripes or grey or brown
                    they follow
Nico's donkey milk cart.

Purring mincing threatening
                    growling
watching waiting
                    The Grecian Cats
guard their ancient realm.

Jennifer Martin

The Chains of Freedom

The tigers that haunt you
emerge at night
They pad on silent paws
across the ghostly bridges
you've burned

Their luminescent eyes
reflect the light
as they prowl in the stark
white shadows

These striped beasts
rattle their chains
as they hunt you down
those endless dark paths

For that which is sought
lies hidden by freedom
as you run from your self:
For the promised land
lies within your soul

∞ ∞ ∞ ∞ ∞ ∞ ∞ ∞ ∞ ∞ ∞ ∞

It matters not
where you lay your head
it's where you
place your heart

Joe Blades

dark age

there was a time   a place and purpose
for writing poems   for aligning earth
with whirling night lights   that big picture
no longer clear   too much background
noise   too much ambient light from cars
and night mirage cities   divers under river ice
search for body of a disappeared son   boyfriend
who slipped (or something) off bridge catwalk
cockroaches feeding on dirty dishes
on bathroom floor   they are always
breeding and almost invisible when small
i am not breeding   near dead   near obsolete
a fish in a cooling ocean without a spark
of plankton creation   without food for thought
without a penny – a near useless copper
for thoughts   and not two cents worth

there was a time for poetry
but now i am hiding in pillows
in my single bed   lights off
except for cyclops red eyes of radios
fire detector and telephone answering machine
my diaphragm vibrating with teenage anger
bounced off shells of atmosphere
this is a dark age
walking ice-slick sidewalks
for sake of walking   for death
defying attraction of poisons
tension in my left knee from sitting
passive   tired as a tethered dog in july sun
with no trees   no dog house   nothing but chain-
scrapped earth and dusted baked lumps
no escape   no rocket pulling
me outside of earth's pull
electrodes wire muscles and brain

Peter Baltensperger

Thirsting

My mind
is filled with images
of thirst:

dried throats,
cracked lips,
fingers
reaching for a mirage.

And others.

Fingers
are always reaching
for mirages:

no reason
to write a poem.

It's the distance
we never quite
understand.

Jeff Seffinga

Somewhere Here

(for Brenda M)

Somewhere the thin slivers of sunshine
carve through a cover of hard snow,
twisting among layers of frozen soil.
They reach the sleeping green memories:
call them to germinate, to recreate
life that gives praise to light and to air.

Somewhere a soft rain begins to fall
in a grey valley, the arid empty place
of dust to which all life must return.
A million cells encased in tough husks
burst from imprisonment and wasteland
is awash in bright colours as water flows.

Here you stand twisting some simple words
into a thin brush, exposing images that
were almost condemned to an empty closet.

Like a shower in the desert you touch dry bones
and call forth rainbows. Like spring sunlight
you carve through old flesh and give it new life.

Donia Blumenfeld Clenman

Melodie

Do you know my melodie?

Blue, like the unquiet sea
Red, like Salome's desire
White, like a virgin star
Green, like torrential spring.

On my birth I sang to her
Yet she always eludes me.
A step ahead. A step behind
Wooing. Surrounding.
      What's the use?
      We are never in tune.

Have you seen my melodie?

The face of a tear-stained child
The laughter of peeling bells
The shadow of a soaring falcon
The transience of myrrh and frankincense.

On my birth I sang to her
Yet she always eludes me.
A skip ahead. A skip behind
Mocking. Surrounding.
      What's the use?
      We are never in tune.

I open my mouth.
Come to roost in the ribcage of my love.
A fever bird. A sun bird.
A bird of prey.
Or just a brown sparrow?
Every melodie is beautiful
When you call her your own.

My tear-stained child!
Come home. I am tired.

                   Salome!
Envelop me with your musky veils.

Sorcerer! Enchanter! Sun Bird!
          Feed on me. Consume me.
          I am your flowering nectar.
                    But stay a while.

Geoffrey St-Pierre

The Eclipse

I'm one to ask what lesson we've to learn
From games the sun and moon have seemed to play.
For mostly each from each have taken turns,
On cue, to dazzle earth with burning day,
Then trade this gold for a milder grey, the sheen
Of silver fur to match a wolfish stare.
Confounded on odd decades may be seen
The roles that each distinct is known to bear:
The moon will lean an edge against the sun
And blacken an hour with light that gives no heat,
Recalling Satan's attempt to overrun
The throne that justly tossed him in defeat.
And now each dusk is offered to our sight
The light of him consigned to rule at night.

Anna Plesums

...just for a smile

This morning as a princess
the sun dressed in a golden gown
and fluttered over the dewed grass
creating a poplar perfumed serenity
as for most formal meeting
with the new day.

But the obnoxious wind
had other thoughts than serenity,
it ripped the clouds like used feathers
and twisted the soil in a wild dances of
Dust Devils.

A cranky day –
the sun isn't making any effort
to give its most to be bright.

I'm longing for the littlest Sun Doggie...

Sonja Dunn

Naming a Dog

When you get a new dog
And it's just a wee pup
And it can't do a thing
'Cept whimper and yup
When you call it to come
But all is in vain
Your job is to give it
A PARTICULAR name
Now the naming of pups
Is a mystical thing
You must choose a name
With an elegant ring
Rover and Spot
Are undignified
And Skippy or Frisky
Would hurt a dog's pride
Remember these names
Are all rather old hat
And be careful your name
Isn't one for a cat
Like Sylvester or Fluffy
Or Grimalkin Fat
Give your dear dog
An unusual moniker
Like Chuckles or Samson
Or Faust or Veronica
Queenie or King would be
Out of the question
But why not Ulysses
Searchmount or Sebastian
If your pup is a Peke
From a land oriental
Sao Ying is a name
That's appropriately gentle
I've met many people

Who have chosen a name
That make their poor dogs
Hang their heads down in shame
There are many grand names
To which puppies will answer
But don't saddle a dog
With Ducks or Merganser
Avoid everyday names
Like Blackie or Sandy
When naming your canine
Choose a handle that's dandy

Lack Styles

How to Drive Your Neighbours Away

Two families live near us, we see them daily too,
they trespass on our yard as if it's theirs, it's true, they do,

They loiter there and boldly stare, intimidate the cats,
they hang around and hang around, two families and their brats

They pay no rent, no mortgage fee, they have no house to lease,
which isn't really very odd because, you see, they're geese.

The big one is the leader, he's a tyrant and a meany
he dominates the other geese, I call him Goosolini.

I stood up on my soap-box and harangued the fowl convention,
heads on pencil-necks popped up, they stood at full attention.

I spoke of revolution, bolshevism and oppression,
told them they were victims of an oligarch aggression.

Told them all of freedom in the proletariat nest,
and even Goosolini blankly stared with all the rest

"Rise up!" I shouted, "rise against this despot now, today!"
they mumbled and they blinked a bit, then shrugged and flapped away.

At this point my belief in goosey suffrage took a blow,
'cause maybe some folks only want their status to be...quo.

J. Alvin Speers

Jumping to Conclusions

The salmon casserole had been prepared
For ladies who would meet that afternoon.
The hostess found her cat helping itself
And chased it to the yard with wooden spoon.

Smoothing the dish where raid was perpetrated,
She served it when the sewing meet was done.
The compliments were many for its flavour
As they partook until it was all gone.

Later, when her guests had all departed,
She went through porch to check for any mail
And saw the body of the cat laying there
With rigor mortis stiff from head to tail.

In panic she called each who had attended
Confessing what events made her perceive,
Urging all to rush down to the hospital
By stomach pump the danger to relieve.

Her husband came home then for supper.
''I met the postman on the street downtown.
He stopped to say he'd rendered us a favour
When he saw our cat had been run down.''

Knowing where the dead pet had made its home,
He retrieved it by the tail like flaming torch
And, not wishing to disturb the ladies' meeting,
Had quietly laid it in the corner of the porch.

Jack Gallach

My Retirement

I thought, I would sleep in
All the time,
Every single day,
But the holiday is over
That cycle has passed,
No more rest now...
The old pattern is back;
The small clock points three in the morning,
The thoughts are fully mine
Not astray, butterflying in the air
So vague that I fantasized and
Didn't know who I was. Freedom...I thought.
Time has caught up with me
And in these wee hours I mourn and
wait...
Will my passion break through?
Not much time left to live
These days...lest
The devil forks me out
for another, last meal.

Jay C. Hershberg

Valentine Bazaar
Rosedale United Church, Feb. 11th 1995

Hand-made objects all around.
Oh, such treasures to be found.
Into a church, I came today,
and found these ''goodies'' on display.
They fairly took my breath away.

With loving words upon some lines
we pass around red valentines.
Emotions, ''deep''? within our souls.
To win some hearts are our goals.
We do adopt such loving roles.

But, only once a year? Too bad!
Whence gone this feeling we once had?
We do, I say with deep regret,
tend to at other times forget,
the love we found when we first met.

I hope, some day, I'll see a change
in thinking we must re-arrange.
Remembering our pledge to be
faithful for all eternity.
Could I but survive, this change to see.

Margaret Houben

There Must be One...

There beyond my reach,
Like a starlit golden beach
On the horizon,
           I know they are there.
My soul has often flown
To where my dreams seem grown.
What strange worlds to find;
           Are they hard or fair?

There must be one, I think,
Where its star rises all pink
Casting hues of red
           On a purple sky.
As it climbs bringing
Warmth to small things clinging
On massive vines,
           Wonders catch my eye.

Here exotic plants
Open to reveal inhabitants
That take to the wind
           With soft throbbing calls.
Now, on the brisk breeze.
Ringing chatter comes to tease
My ears: such queer
           Noisy caterwauls!

A fragrance in the air
All spiced and sweet and rare
Tells me of flowers,
           Fresh fruit, and of life.
Warm earth on bare feet,
The shade of giant trees ease the heat
As the horizon cuts
           The sun like a knife.

The contented sighs
As the flyers bid goodbyes
To each other;
            The plants gently close.
With the heaven's drapery
Of tatted stars a canopy,
I rejoice to join
            One planet's repose.

Linda Frank

Wisteria

We harboured one of the oldest wisterias
in Hamilton, until it snaked its selfish
body around its host, a stoic mountain ash
without whose benevolence the wisteria
could not have attained its elder status

The vine squeezed the tree gaunt, wrung
the sap right out of the ash, until
unable to sustain the two
of them any longer, the ash surrendered,
leaked its last breath cored through the rigid
rows of woodpecker holes
so neatly knocked into its bark

And yielded in one final
bow, branches and leaves
sweeping the ground in graceful farewell,
forsaking the wisteria to scream
in selfish indignation, sensing
it could not endure alone, conscious
of the horror it had wrought upon itself

So intermingled were they one with the other
that the wisteria too was uprooted before its time
It bloomed in vain, preened in vain,
was pruned in vain – or so we thought

We mourned the wisteria for the loss
of its glory, its livid damson bounty
the centuries within the forest of its trunks
we mourned the ash for its majesty
and globular orange contributions
to the drunken state of spring birds

But wisteria – wisteria perseveres
Wicked grin along its skinny new tendrils,
persistent, it prowls back out of its death bed,
creeps out of the coffin stump of ash,
thrusting tentacle limbs once again
to the sky, writhing for a new host

Norma West Linder

Dark Visions

Under the 60-watt bulb
of his ugly furnished room
each new rebuff
in his adopted city
blossomed into a poem

When he had created
2 dozen long-stemmed beauties
he mailed his bouquet
to a local publisher
went to work happy

Tonight he returned dog tired
dead sick of dirty dishes
to find his rejected roses
in the foyer mail box

He went straight up
to his room
but he didn't turn on
the light

James Deahl

Ulysses & Myrtle

Ulysses Grant Deahl

In time I came to run the local mine –
in partnership with others, I might add.
I sent several of my sons to college
and saw that all but one escaped the pits.
The house is mine. That great stone wall out front
was built by me and my boys to restrain
the yard and its yellow rose Myrtle loved.

They're all dead now, but they were tough; Jup, Ken,
and Warren survived the slaughter to
father sons. I count myself lucky for that;
other men watched their boys vanish in
the mud and gas of France. And my grandson
reads my Bible every night. I've earned my peace.

Myrtle Virginia Cale Deahl

What did I know of men? My daddy died
when I was three; momma lived a widow
her last days. I was just a dreamy schoolgirl
when Ulysses took me to wife and,
after Velma died, his driving rhythm
kept me pregnant until fresh youth was spent.
Yet I kept my figure to die as slim

as on our wedding day. Oh, how I missed
those things my schoolmates took for granted:
families loving and complete, time to live
before the babies came. Now grandchildren
I never got to know race around those
roses I laboured hard to raise and grow.

Carol Harrington

Gibbon's Park, London, 1992.

This vast green paddock
Stretches away for ever,
Inspiring, refreshing
All who come for air.
The stalwart trees and shrubs
Are like an army at rest,
Ready to succour and defend
Quietly, calmly, softly.

The great aloneness of the soul
Then rises up above the trees
And rests triumphant in the beauty.

I.B. Iskov

election day or uncle bobby

the discriminating clown
floats on parade
around city hall
lined with people
watching
the bulbous crimson flag
sail among billowy white clouds
of fallout

the audience
lifts their voices high
to circle the Head
of the beanbag raggedy creature
filled with sawdust

kissing babies
passing out balloons
full of empty promises
dancing for votes
on university

Ted Plantos

Born Thomas D'Arcy McGee

Carlingford, Ireland

Born to a daughter of Dublin on a Wednesday in April, 1825
Delivered wailing to the leafy wet spring
while the thrashing green of the Irish Sea
roared north to the Channel and beyond
Atlantic winds on Rosstrevor Coast
wetted the breath of grass and ferns
And Thomas D'Arcy McGee, he of "good old rebel blood,"
breathed his first in Ireland's light

George Bernstein

Winter Apocalypse

Fragments of the dead
Like ghostly vapour trails
Dance their solemn way
      To the beginning,
      And the end.

Death roars and sighs in
A cacophony of deafening silence
      Trumpets blast
      A double-deuteronomy
      Alarm.
      The last
      of days.

The celestial top spins
Through beckoning buds and
Summer green
And autumn brown. Then
Sheathed in frosty armour
Anchored to clanging groans
Pitching and yawing in
A sea of seething snow
It drowns in icy froth
As volcanic bubbles echo a
Mournful windblown dirge.
      Flame and ash
      Ash and ice
      The end of days.

Despair grins
From faceless shadows
Fused in the gaunt
Glazed concrete sphinx.

Aeons ago
Nebulae of fiery cloud
Blossomed into earthy splendour.

Will the promise of its glory
Be shattered
By the sons of Cain?

Elizabeth St Jacques

Three Haiku

grandmother kneading
song and prayer
into our daily bread

grandfather's cackle
filling wicker baskets
...warm brown eggs

on the farm
under grandma's quilt, a dream
of wild-eyed geese

Allan Briesmaster

Late Night Garden

Airless room; ...hot wool.
No breath strains through the screens from
the garden.

Toward our flowerbed gate
over city's hazy rumble
lean a few moist stars.

Below electric
peachdown cloud   our small orchard's
green mounds huddle, black.

Petalled darkness
crush low, till we brush their cheeks,
shadows to shadow.

Soft names are opening:
"snow-on-the-mountain," high pink "phlox,"
feathery "cosmos"...

Night's last embers   drop;
inner blooms flare up through each
handheld aroma.

Pale smudges, dark scents
lift, and a sweet smoke trails   off
the cooling torches.

We drift, calmed and buoyed
with the mix of nightbreaths, onto our
own wide bed's raft.

Joachim K. Baum

Homestead on the Hill

Sublime and lonely on the hill
stands the weather-beaten homestead, still.
This little wooden house, so hassle-free,
ever having a wide-spread view,
and the Summer sky infinite blue,
merges on the horizon with the sea.

At night, when the mist floated from below,
making tattered night-shadows grow.
A drifting, misty veil, never to stay,
for one gust of wind could wash it away.
But then, it would come to play again,
putting the shadow-game in night's view.

Even today, I see them still:
the moon-shadows, a beautiful sight,
from the little old house on the hill,
peaceful and warm on a starlit night.
But short of life as pretty blossoms must,
so are we; and the old house turned to dust.

Herb Barrett

Wishful Thinking

If we should restrain those hands
Moving inexorably across the face of time
Freeze to immobility
The Rich canvas of our flesh...
What startling revelation
Might that incident disclose?

      A deadpan look
      Of lascivious living
      A leering stare
      Of utter estrangement
      An implied and constant threat
      Of violence and hostility...

Were that wish
Unequivocally granted
Might it not prove to be
too unbearable to sustain?

      Might it also reveal
      Some eager faces
      Uplifted to an ancient star
      Caught in that awesome moment
      Their eyes still bright
      With humanity and meaning!

Jennifer Footman

Vivarium: when the Doctor in Emerg said there were Other ways of Dealing with her Problems

Those who are blind seem to believe
they can show the use of the white stick.

Those who are deaf seem to believe
they can help us hear the music of joy

Salt seasons the bones of her body, orchards
don't spring out of cracked asphalt.

She has become familiar with the curl
on the face of the lizard.

When the lizard smiles, it's a true smile.
He folds hours to suit his skin,

picks to drop his tail in his own good time.
He lives the life of a good reptile

lizarding about, flicking things from his path
leaving trails in the dust of the shelf

where she keeps her sentimental what-nots,
precious memories for an old age.

He smashes them. After all, they mean
nothing to him, nothing in the reptile world.

Michael Wurster

After the Flooding

I was travelling on foot through a neighbourhood near my own
after the flooding. I was travelling with a small grey cat
named Sappho. Sometimes she would walk beside me, sometimes
I would carry her. When she walked, she would move about
exploring, discovering things.

We wound up entering a house and were there some time,
encountered one of two sisters just before we got away.
One of the sisters had lost the use of her legs, but exhibited
a sensuality that reminded of the flooding, such intense
and lyric power. We were on the floor in the upstairs parlour
when the other came in and caught us. She was pissed off.
Negotiation.

Why didn't the first philosopher want to go on living? They
sat in a white room and discussed it, the facts of the palpable
world, how she was moaning, the two of us in ecstasy on that
parlour floor. These two sisters were blonde. I insist on it.
The one without the use of her legs was fleshy. She may not
have been a true blonde. Who stops to count?

Sappho discoursed on these events from the maple tree outside.

Winona Baker

A Haiku Seasonal

The bear in the blossoms
holds out his arms
I do not understand

ninety-year old nun
sells ceramic babies –
at the spring bazaar

prize sweetpeas
where the outhouse was emptied
last spring

shore birds rise
pulling the waves in
drop the waves retreat

election rally
purple loosestrife spreads
along the river

in the stubble
a ball of blue wool
unwinds in the wind

the old dog
chained in the back yard
barks coldly

white-breathed hooker
stares in the window
at the wedding gown

Afterword

I have always had very special feelings for the Canadian Poetry Association. During the autumn of 1994 my first full-size poetry collection, *No Cold Ash*, was published. My old friend and fellow poet Chris Faiers set me up with a reading at the Main Street branch of the Toronto Public Library. After the reading we all went off to The Balmy Arms, a tavern by the shore of Lake Ontario. It was the first (and last) time I ever bought a round for the house. It was that kind of night.

As the hours passed there was much bitching and many a complaint about the state of poetry in Canada. We saw a need for a poetry organization that would put the *poem* first. All too often, poetry organizations would focus their efforts on promoting the egos and careers of poets, while the poem itself was almost neglected. Suddenly, Wayne Ray slapped $5 on the table and declared, "I found the Canadian Poetry Association!" And so it was. This was on January 16, 1985. Now ten years have gone by and the CPA is still in business; more importantly, it is still putting the poem first.

A number of us, cash in hand, signed up. In addition to our founder, Wayne Ray, about ten of us joined on the spot or within a few days. These charter members included Shaunt Basmajian, Susan Ioannou, Bev Daurio, Mark Gordon, Ted Plantos, Chris Faiers, Jones, Dale Loucareas, Mary Ellen Csamer, and myself. Wayne became the first Chairman of the CPA and Chris served as our Recording Secretary.

In almost no time at all (and I'm still not sure how Wayne, Chris, and Shaunt managed the job) we had members from Newfoundland to British Columbia, as well as in the United States and Great Britain. Then, all of a sudden, there was a chapter in London run by Sheila Martindale as well as one in Hamilton, where Jeff Seffinga and Herb Barrett kept things cooking. By the time the CPA was two years old, Milton Acorn had joined and there were chapters being established from Nova Scotia to British Columbia.

But what was the CPA's reason for existing? (One should note that almost all of the charter members were members of The League of Canadian Poets, the Canadian Authors Association, or some other literary group.) On March 5, 1985 Shaunt wrote an open letter to our members and other interested persons:

> As an organization, to most of us that were there that evening [January 16, 1985], it was basically agreed our main objective for the group would be to promote a broader exposure of poetry to the general public and hopefully develop into an international connection for Canadian

poets. We also agreed we would work in harmony with other groups and organizations . . .

The CPA was to welcome everyone – poets, readers of poetry, booksellers, teachers, librarians, editors – everyone with an interest in poetry. Importantly, there was to be no hierarchy of membership. No senior members, no junior members, no associate members. From Milton Acorn to the high school scribbler, we were all members, plain and simple. To continue Shaunt's statement:

> . . . it wasn't until recently that an honest effort was made by Wayne Ray
> to finally start a group that would once and for all represent all poets and
> non-poets alike, openly and democratically in one organization regardless
> of personal bias, publication criteria, professional capability.

To this day the CPA embraces all types of poetry, from the most experimental forms of L=A=N=G=U=A=G=E poetry to the New Formalism. It is, however, true that a number of poets who have played significant roles in the CPA have come out of People's Poetry. Our first Life Member was Milton Acorn. And such prominent people's poets as Ted Plantos, Susan Ioannou, Chris Faiers, John B. Lee, and Tom Wayman have helped identify the CPA with mainline Canadian poetry.

Over the last decade, the CPA has attracted a number of movers and shapers of our literary culture. The owners of several leading publishing houses have been active CPAers: Broken Jaw Press, HMS Press, The Mercury Press, Moonstone Press, Ouroboros, Pottersfield Press, River City Press, South Western Ontario Poetry, and Unfinished Monument Press.

And CPA members have edited some of the most influential literary periodicals: *Arc, Breakthrough! Magazine, Canadian Author, Cross-Canada Writers' Magazine, Daybreak, Issue One* (England), *Mainichi Daily News* (Japan), *New Cicada* (Japan), *New Muse of Contempt, paragraph, Poetry Canada Review, Poetry Halifax Dartmouth, The Pottersfield Portfolio, Rampike, St. Thomas Chronicles, Tidepool, Waves,* and *Writ.*

From the above lists it should be clear that CPA members represent the whole spectrum of poetry in Canada. We do not exist to promote any one school, literary movement, or set of regional concerns. For example, most national writing groups have almost half of their members within the greater Toronto area. I think it is interesting that only 30% of CPA members reside in the Toronto area. The CPA actually has more members in small towns than in Toronto: and that, I believe, makes us unique.

The CPA remains true to Shaunt's statement. We are democratic, member-controlled, and open. There are no backroom boys, no secret factions, no hidden agendas. We have never had a feminist caucus because we have never been a sexist organization. We have a tradition of active women who have been important in the development of the CPA. And the CPA has always had members who (for want of a better term) are representatives of various racial and ethnic groups. We have never had to fight racism because we have not been racist. If you need poetry in your life we want you to join. All are welcome.

Although he was not a charter member, one poet who was a great help during our early days was Milton Acorn (1923-1986). Milton, always a strong supporter of the aims and objectives of the CPA, was appointed a Life Member shortly before his death. Here is a poem he wrote at that time.

It's All in Mother's Head

for Helen Carbonell Acorn, 1900-1984

It's all in mother's head that she can dance.
At seventy-nine that's just ridiculous.
But when the band commences purblind romance,
Spinning dizzy on a dizzy record,
Her eyes begin to burn and feet to tap.
Hands work an invisible accordion,
Till presently she's up with some assistance,
Like a tall ship heaving out its sails
Despite the wallops of the waves and tide
To convert the elements' resistance.

It's all in mother's head that she can glide
Unerringly through the erring couples.
All the able partners with whom she doubled
Are gone to ground or anchored to their chairs
Till she alone, to hand applause and cheers,
Reels reels that are reels in every sense known –
Really doing it, still vast and full-blown,
Red-headed as ever a head was red.
Risen she is, but not from the dead;
From hopes that were false to hopes that are true,

From pert old-fashioned steps that seem to slide
As one cloud seems to coast upon another
In a cloggish and half-clumsy ride,
As a lupine bitch, leader of the pack,
Gets with each step just a whisht of a catch;
Sets each foot to raise it in all pride.

Each completed figure draws all breath
Out of a line of steam locomotives
Climbing the Rockies at a bawling crawl,
Or an ocean liner rolling all
The storm with it while fully figurative.
The eyes to watch her and the hands to catch
Would never let the floorboards hit her ass.
They fit too sure, are too well nailed for that:
Until after some moments she collapses
With a cry of "How's that? How did I do?"
"Just fine our lady! Great-grandmother you!"
All in her head, but there's the evidence.

(reprinted from *The Uncollected Acorn*
Toronto, Deneau Publishers, 1987)

It is a great pleasure to be able to include this Acorn poem. And it is also a pleasure to note how many members who were with us ten years ago – Ted Plantos, Susan Ioannou, Wayne Ray, Sonja Dunn, Jeff Seffinga, Rosemary Aubert, Michael Wurster, Peter Baltensperger, Margaret Houben, Albert W.J. Harper, and the late Herb Barrett – have contributed work to this anthology in celebration of the first decade of the CPA.

Martin Singleton once noted that making a poem was difficult magic. The poet starts with little more that a limited (for it can only be so) understanding of language and an observation or idea. It can really be said that the poet makes something out of nothing, like coaxing a Maritime dance tune from an invisible accordion.

– James Deahl
President, Canadian Poetry Association

Contributors

Melvin Robert Appell lives in London, Ontario with Sufi, the cat, and very dear friend, Anne.

Beryl Baigent was born in North Wales. Her most recent book is *Hiraeth: In Search of Celtic Origins*, a 25 year selection from previous books and new poems.

Winona Baker has authored three haiku collections, two poetry books, and her poetry has appeared in periodicals and over 30 anthologies from around the world.

Peter Baltensperger is the author of six volumes of poetry, including *Arcana for a Silent Voice* (Mercury Press). He is currently publisher of Moonstone Press in Goderich, Ontario.

Herb Barrett was born, educated, and lived in Hamilton, Ontario, He conducted poetry groups for over 40 years, edited *Tidepool* for 11 years, and authored three books.

Jill Battson is an international poet perhaps best known as producer of the *Word Up* poetry video project for MuchMusic. She is an author of *Playing in The Asphalt Garden* (Insomniac Press).

Joachim K. Baum, born 1935, grew up in Niederlausitz, East Germany. He has published poetry books in English and German, including, *Fur meine Heimat aus der Ferne*.

George Bernstein is an orthopaedic Surgeon practising in Windsor, Ontario. He has published short stories, poems, essays and book reviews in Canadian and American journals.

Joe Blades is a writer, artist and publisher living in Fredericton, New Brunswick. A recent poetry chapbook of his is *Rummaging for Rhinos* (Pooka Press).

Margaret Joy Borle is a writer living in rural Alberta. She has published in periodicals, anthologies and a 1993 collection, *Dark Singing*.

Allan Briesmaster is a poet/writer, and host of the Art Bar Wednesday Night Poetry Series in Toronto, where he lives with his wife and daughter.

Carla Campoli graduated from UofT in 1995 with a B.A. in French and Italian, and is also an accomplished pianist, music teacher, organist and cantor of her local parish.

Mary Chryssoulakis, born in Montreal, has resided in Sarnia since 1957. Her short stories, articles and poetry have been published in magazines and anthologies in Canada and Bermuda.

Donia Blumenfeld Clenman was born in Poland and has lived in Toronto since 1948. Her most recent books are *Older and in Love* and *A Scroll of Remembrance* (Flowerfield and Littleman).

James Deahl is the author of more than a dozen literary titles including *Under the Watchful Eye: Poetry and Discourse* (Broken Jaw Press).

Mary Lou Doyon, from Sarnia, Ontario started writing poetry as a legacy to her children.

Bernadette Dyer is a poet, artist, storyteller and short story writer living in Toronto Her poem ''Masks'' has won a 1995 Canadian League of Black Artists, Inc. Competition.

Bob Ezergailis has lost count of the number of poems he has written and published.

Penny L. Ferguson lives and writes in Truro, Nova Scotia where she edits *The Amethyst Review*.

p.j. flaming, from Alberta, author of *voir dire* (Broken Jaw Press), is the 1995/96 Writer-in-Residence for the Dumfries and Galloway Region of southwest Scotland.

Suzanne Fitz-Andrews, of Etobicoke, has been writing poetry since the age of nine. She works as an almost sane systems analyst by day and as an almost mad poet by night.

Jennifer Footman is a Brampton poet who originated in India and came to Canada via the U.K.

Jill Meriel Fox lives in Cambridge, Ontario where she operates a genealogical business. She has published poems in numerous periodicals and anthologies.

Linda Frank was born in Montreal and lives in Hamilton, Ontario. She has published poetry in journals, and is presently under contract to write a sociology textbook, due out in 1998.

Kathy Fretwell, born in NYC, lives in Parry Sound. Has published *The Ultimate Contact* and *Apple, Worm, and All* (Fiddlehead Poetry Books). And in magazines and anthologies.

Lini Richarda Grol is from the Netherlands and living Brampton, Ontario. She has published poetry, prose and illustrations in Holland, South Africa, Belgium, U.K., US and Canada.

Carol Harrington was born in Yorkshire, England and grew up in Edinburgh, Scotland. Carol her husband and two sons live in London, Ontario, where she started writing.

Jay C. Hershberg was born and grew up in Winnipeg. After being in the air force in WWII, he raised his family, and started writing and publishing poetry.

Darlene Spong Henderson was born and raised in London, Ontario. She and her family have resided in St. Albert, Alberta since 1979. Darlene writes poetry and short stories.

Margaret Houben lives in B.C. Her poetry has appeared in several anthologies and a chapbook.

Sheila Hyland writes poetry and prose, and has published three poetry collections.

Guna Ikona is a Latvian-Canadian poet who has published several volumes of her work. She is also the literary and art editor of the Latvian global magazine, *DV*.

John B. Lee is the only two-time winner of the Milton Acorn Memorial People's Poet Award, also won the 1995 Tilden/CBC Radio/Saturday Night Literary Award for Poetry.

Bernice Lever has authored nine books including *The Waiting Room* (Highway Book Shop).

Norma West Linder has authored over a dozen books including poetry, novels and memoirs.

Maynard Luterman is a practising physician in London, Ontario and father of two daughters. Originally from Montreal, he studied at John Hopkins University and McGill Medical School.

Jennifer Martin is a single parent, educator, published author of educational materials and a poet in Manotick, Ontario.

Hilton McCully's autumn '95 book is *Pictou Island (BHA E CHO SNOG)*. Having retired after 36 years of teaching, he lives in Dartmouth, Nova Scotia.

Hope Morritt has published three novels, two nonfiction books, and poetry collections including *Soldier Come Home.*

Mary Partridge's work has appeared in literary magazines and newspapers in Canada, the United States and Japan. She lives in Elliot Lake, Ontario.

Ted Plantos has published ten poetry books and two children's books. Recent books are *Mosquito Nirvana* (Wolsak and Wynn) and *Dogs Know about Parades* (Black Moss).

Anna Plesums, born in Latvia, lives in Egbert, Ontario. At 70, she is still a working caregiver.

Wayne Ray is a poet, publisher, and National Coordinator of the C.P.A. in London, Ontario.

Jeff Seffinga was born in the Netherlands but grew up in eastern Ontario. He has authored three poetry collections, and recently was a member of the jazz/poetry collective "Naked on Stage."

Gail Sidonie Sobat has published in numerous periodicals including *Other Voices, Secrets from the Orange Couch*, and *The Amethyst Review.*

J. Alvin Speers is an Alberta author, poet, editor and publisher. Has authored sixteen books.

Gerry Stewart has published in over 100 magazines. He is also a saxophonist and working musician. Originally from Liverpool, Gerry is now kicking his heels over in Mississauga.

Elizabeth St Jacques has published several books of poetry, including *Around the Tree of Light* (maplebud press). She lives in Sault Ste. Marie, Ontario.

Geoffrey St-Pierre currently is a schoolteacher in Chibougamau, in northwestern Quebec.

Isabel Sturgeon is a Canadian artist who studied in Europe, the Yukon Territory and at the Ottawa School of Art. She has published in magazine and anthologies.

Lack Styles is a videotape editor by trade, and a musician and bathroom poet by nature. His poetry has appeared in periodicals and anthologies, and on CBC.

Lynn Tait, of Sarnia, considers herself a full-time poet and a part-time school bus driver who has published in Canada and the US.

Adele Kearns Thomas, originally from Quebec, is president of the Sarnia C.A.A. branch.

Heather Tisdale-Nisbet lives in Nepean, Ontario. Her poetry is published in several magazines.

Anne F. Walker, of Toronto, is the author of *Pregnant Poems* (Black Moss Press).

Michael Wurster, a founding member of Pittsburgh Poetry Exchange, teaches at Pittsburgh Centre for the Arts School. His collection is *The Cruelty of the Desert* (Cottage Wordsmiths).